Le$$on Ledgers

by Christine Hadlock

ISBN: 978-1981371808

Student Information

Name	Age	Birthday	Parents	Phone/Text	Email

SPENDING CATEGORIES

A= Advertising
B= Books
E= Education
G=Gifts
I= Instruments/Repair/Tuning
M= Music
O= Office Supplies
P= Prizes
R= Recitals
S=Sound Equipment/Recording
T= Taxes/Accounting
Misc.= Miscellaneous

Annual Expense Log

Date	Description	Amount	Spending Category	Payment Method	(Enter Total Only) Monthly Expenses	(Enter Total Monthly) Annual Expenses To Date

SPENDING CATEGORIES

A= Advertising	I= Instruments/Repair/Tuning	R= Recitals
B= Books	M= Music	S=Sound Equipment/Recording
E= Education	O= Office Supplies	T= Taxes/Accounting
G=Gifts	P= Prizes	Misc.= Miscellaneous

Annual Expense Log

Date	Description	Amount	Spending Category	Payment Method	(Enter Total Only) Monthly Expenses	(Enter Total Monthly) Annual Expenses To Date

SPENDING CATEGORIES

A= Advertising
B= Books
E= Education
G=Gifts
I= Instruments/Repair/Tuning
M= Music
O= Office Supplies
P= Prizes
R= Recitals
S=Sound Equipment/Recording
T= Taxes/Accounting
Misc.= Miscellaneous

Annual Expense Log

Date	Description	Amount	Spending Category	Payment Method	(Enter Total Only) Monthly Expenses	(Enter Total Monthly) Annual Expenses To Date

SPENDING CATEGORIES
A= Advertising I= Instruments/Repair/Tuning R= Recitals
B= Books M= Music S=Sound Equipment/Recording
E= Education O= Office Supplies T= Taxes/Accounting
G=Gifts P= Prizes Misc.= Miscellaneous

Annual Expense Log

Date	Description	Amount	Spending Category	Payment Method	(Enter Total Only) Monthly Expenses	(Enter Total Monthly) Annual Expenses To Date

SPENDING CATEGORIES

A= Advertising
B= Books
E= Education
G=Gifts
I= Instruments/Repair/Tuning
M= Music
O= Office Supplies
P= Prizes
R= Recitals
S=Sound Equipment/Recording
T= Taxes/Accounting
Misc.= Miscellaneous

Annual Expense Log

Date	Description	Amount	Spending Category	Payment Method	(Enter Total Only) Monthly Expenses	(Enter Total Monthly) Annual Expenses To Date

SPENDING CATEGORIES

A= Advertising
B= Books
E= Education
G=Gifts
I= Instruments/Repair/Tuning
M= Music
O= Office Supplies
P= Prizes
R= Recitals
S=Sound Equipment/Recording
T= Taxes/Accounting
Misc.= Miscellaneous

Annual Expense Log

Date	Description	Amount	Spending Category	Payment Method	(Enter Total Only) Monthly Expenses	(Enter Total Monthly) Annual Expenses To Date

January 2018

Monthly Income & Bank Deposits

Anticipated Income	Student	Actual Income	Date Deposited	(Enter Tally Only) Deposit Total	(Enter Tally Only) Monthly Income	(Enter Tally Only) Annual Income To Date

February 2018

Monthly Income & Bank Deposits

Anticipated Income	Student	Actual Income	Date Deposited	(Enter Tally Only) Deposit Total	(Enter Tally Only) Monthly Income	(Enter Tally Only) Annual Income To Date

March 2018

Monthly Income & Bank Deposits

Anticipated Income	Student	Actual Income	Date Deposited	(Enter Tally Only) Deposit Total	(Enter Tally Only) Monthly Income	(Enter Tally Only) Annual Income To Date

April 2018

Monthly Income & Bank Deposits

Anticipated Income	Student	Actual Income	Date Deposited	(Enter Tally Only) Deposit Total	(Enter Tally Only) Monthly Income	(Enter Tally Only) Annual Income To Date

May 2018

Monthly Income & Bank Deposits

Anticipated Income	Student	Actual Income	Date Deposited	(Enter Tally Only) Deposit Total	(Enter Tally Only) Monthly Income	(Enter Tally Only) Annual Income To Date

June 2018

Monthly Income & Bank Deposits

Anticipated Income	Student	Actual Income	Date Deposited	(Enter Tally Only) Deposit Total	(Enter Tally Only) Monthly Income	(Enter Tally Only) Annual Income To Date

July 2018

Monthly Income & Bank Deposits

Anticipated Income	Student	Actual Income	Date Deposited	(Enter Tally Only) Deposit Total	(Enter Tally Only) Monthly Income	(Enter Tally Only) Annual Income To Date

August 2018

Monthly Income & Bank Deposits

Anticipated Income	Student	Actual Income	Date Deposited	(Enter Tally Only) Deposit Total	(Enter Tally Only) Monthly Income	(Enter Tally Only) Annual Income To Date

September 2018

Monthly Income & Bank Deposits

Anticipated Income	Student	Actual Income	Date Deposited	(Enter Tally Only) Deposit Total	(Enter Tally Only) Monthly Income	(Enter Tally Only) Annual Income To Date

October 2018

Monthly Income & Bank Deposits

Anticipated Income	Student	Actual Income	Date Deposited	(Enter Tally Only) Deposit Total	(Enter Tally Only) Monthly Income	(Enter Tally Only) Annual Income To Date

November 2018

Monthly Income & Bank Deposits

Anticipated Income	Student	Actual Income	Date Deposited	(Enter Tally Only) Deposit Total	(Enter Tally Only) Monthly Income	(Enter Tally Only) Annual Income To Date

December 2018

Monthly Income & Bank Deposits

Anticipated Income	Student	Actual Income	Date Deposited	(Enter Tally Only) Deposit Total	(Enter Tally Only) Monthly Income	(Enter Tally Only) Annual Income To Date

Spring Schedule

TIME	MONDAY	TUESDAY	WEDNESDAY	THURSDAY	FRIDAY	SATURDAY
6:00						
6:30						
7:00						
7:30						
8:00						
8:30						
9:00						
9:30						
10:00						
10:30						
11:00						
11:30						
12:00						
12:30						
1:00						
1:30						
2:00						
2:30						
3:00						
3:30						
4:00						
4:30						
5:00						
5:30						
6:00						
6:30						
7:00						
7:30						

Summer Schedule

TIME	MONDAY	TUESDAY	WEDNESDAY	THURSDAY	FRIDAY	SATURDAY
6:00						
6:30						
7:00						
7:30						
8:00						
8:30						
9:00						
9:30						
10:00						
10:30						
11:00						
11:30						
12:00						
12:30						
1:00						
1:30						
2:00						
2:30						
3:00						
3:30						
4:00						
4:30						
5:00						
5:30						
6:00						
6:30						
7:00						
7:30						

Fall Schedule

TIME	MONDAY	TUESDAY	WEDNESDAY	THURSDAY	FRIDAY	SATURDAY
6:00						
6:30						
7:00						
7:30						
8:00						
8:30						
9:00						
9:30						
10:00						
10:30						
11:00						
11:30						
12:00						
12:30						
1:00						
1:30						
2:00						
2:30						
3:00						
3:30						
4:00						
4:30						
5:00						
5:30						
6:00						
6:30						
7:00						
7:30						

January 2018

Lesson Log

	STUDENT NAME	Payment Amount / Date / Description	1stWeek			2nd Week			3rd Week			4th Week			5th Week		
			Date	Present	Absent	Date	Present	Absent	Date	Present	Absent	Date	Present	Absent	Date	Present	Absent
1																	
2																	
3																	
4																	
5																	
6																	
7																	
8																	
9																	
10																	
11																	
12																	
13																	
14																	
15																	
16																	
17																	
18																	
19																	
20																	
21																	
22																	

February 2018

Lesson Log

	STUDENT NAME	Payment Amount / Date / Description	1st Week			2nd Week			3rd Week			4th Week			5th Week		
			Date	Present	Absent	Date	Present	Absent	Date	Present	Absent	Date	Present	Absent	Date	Present	Absent
1																	
2																	
3																	
4																	
5																	
6																	
7																	
8																	
9																	
10																	
11																	
12																	
13																	
14																	
15																	
16																	
17																	
18																	
19																	
20																	
21																	
22																	

March 2018

Lesson Log

	STUDENT NAME	Payment Amount / Date / Description	1stWeek			2nd Week			3rd Week			4th Week			5th Week		
			Date	Present	Absent	Date	Present	Absent	Date	Present	Absent	Date	Present	Absent	Date	Present	Absent
1																	
2																	
3																	
4																	
5																	
6																	
7																	
8																	
9																	
10																	
11																	
12																	
13																	
14																	
15																	
16																	
17																	
18																	
19																	
20																	
21																	
22																	

April 2018

Lesson Log

	STUDENT NAME	Payment Amount / Date / Description	1st Week			2nd Week			3rd Week			4th Week			5th Week		
			Date	Present	Absent	Date	Present	Absent	Date	Present	Absent	Date	Present	Absent	Date	Present	Absent
1																	
2																	
3																	
4																	
5																	
6																	
7																	
8																	
9																	
10																	
11																	
12																	
13																	
14																	
15																	
16																	
17																	
18																	
19																	
20																	
21																	
22																	

May 2018

Lesson Log

	STUDENT NAME	Payment Amount / Date / Description	1stWeek			2nd Week			3rd Week			4th Week			5th Week		
			Date	Present	Absent	Date	Present	Absent	Date	Present	Absent	Date	Present	Absent	Date	Present	Absent
1																	
2																	
3																	
4																	
5																	
6																	
7																	
8																	
9																	
10																	
11																	
12																	
13																	
14																	
15																	
16																	
17																	
18																	
19																	
20																	
21																	
22																	

June 2018

Lesson Log

	STUDENT NAME	Payment Amount / Date / Description	1st Week			2nd Week			3rd Week			4th Week			5th Week		
			Date	Present	Absent	Date	Present	Absent	Date	Present	Absent	Date	Present	Absent	Date	Present	Absent
1																	
2																	
3																	
4																	
5																	
6																	
7																	
8																	
9																	
10																	
11																	
12																	
13																	
14																	
15																	
16																	
17																	
18																	
19																	
20																	
21																	
22																	

July 2018

Lesson Log

	STUDENT NAME	Payment Amount / Date / Description	1stWeek			2nd Week			3rd Week			4th Week			5th Week		
			Date	Present	Absent	Date	Present	Absent	Date	Present	Absent	Date	Present	Absent	Date	Present	Absent
1																	
2																	
3																	
4																	
5																	
6																	
7																	
8																	
9																	
10																	
11																	
12																	
13																	
14																	
15																	
16																	
17																	
18																	
19																	
20																	
21																	
22																	

August 2018

Lesson Log

	STUDENT NAME	Payment Amount / Date / Description	1st Week			2nd Week			3rd Week			4th Week			5th Week		
			Date	Present	Absent	Date	Present	Absent	Date	Present	Absent	Date	Present	Absent	Date	Present	Absent
1																	
2																	
3																	
4																	
5																	
6																	
7																	
8																	
9																	
10																	
11																	
12																	
13																	
14																	
15																	
16																	
17																	
18																	
19																	
20																	
21																	
22																	

September 2018

Lesson Log

	STUDENT NAME	Payment Amount / Date / Description	1stWeek			2nd Week			3rd Week			4th Week			5th Week		
			Date	Present	Absent	Date	Present	Absent	Date	Present	Absent	Date	Present	Absent	Date	Present	Absent
1																	
2																	
3																	
4																	
5																	
6																	
7																	
8																	
9																	
10																	
11																	
12																	
13																	
14																	
15																	
16																	
17																	
18																	
19																	
20																	
21																	
22																	

October 2018

Lesson Log

	STUDENT NAME	Payment Amount / Date / Description	1st Week			2nd Week			3rd Week			4th Week			5th Week		
			Date	Present	Absent	Date	Present	Absent	Date	Present	Absent	Date	Present	Absent	Date	Present	Absent
1																	
2																	
3																	
4																	
5																	
6																	
7																	
8																	
9																	
10																	
11																	
12																	
13																	
14																	
15																	
16																	
17																	
18																	
19																	
20																	
21																	
22																	

November 2018

Lesson Log

	STUDENT NAME	Payment Amount / Date / Description	1stWeek			2nd Week			3rd Week			4th Week			5th Week		
			Date	Present	Absent	Date	Present	Absent	Date	Present	Absent	Date	Present	Absent	Date	Present	Absent
1																	
2																	
3																	
4																	
5																	
6																	
7																	
8																	
9																	
10																	
11																	
12																	
13																	
14																	
15																	
16																	
17																	
18																	
19																	
20																	
21																	
22																	

December 2018

Lesson Log

	STUDENT NAME	Payment Amount / Date / Description	1st Week			2nd Week			3rd Week			4th Week			5th Week		
			Date	Present	Absent	Date	Present	Absent	Date	Present	Absent	Date	Present	Absent	Date	Present	Absent
1																	
2																	
3																	
4																	
5																	
6																	
7																	
8																	
9																	
10																	
11																	
12																	
13																	
14																	
15																	
16																	
17																	
18																	
19																	
20																	
21																	
22																	

Student Progress Plans & Reports

Date	Name	Goals	Focus Skills	Notes

Student Progress Plans & Reports

Date	Name	Goals	Focus Skills	Notes

Date	Name	Goals	Focus Skills	Notes

Student Progress Plans & Reports

Date	Name	Goals	Focus Skills	Notes

Student Progress Plans & Reports

Date	Name	Goals	Focus Skills	Notes

Student Progress Plans & Reports

Date	Name	Goals	Focus Skills	Notes

Student Progress Plans & Reports

Date	Name	Goals	Focus Skills	Notes

Student Progress Plans & Reports

Date	Name	Goals	Focus Skills	Notes

Spring Recital

Student	Recital Pieces	Note-Ready	Memorized	Performance Ready with Dynamics

Fall Recital

Student	Recital Pieces	Note-Ready	Memorized	Performance Ready with Dynamics

Winter Recital

Student	Recital Pieces	Note-Ready	Memorized	Performance Ready with Dynamics

January 2018

Sunday	Monday	Tuesday	Wednesday	Thursday	Friday	Saturday
	1 New Year's Day	2	3	4	5	6
7	8	9	10	11	12	13
14	15 M. Luther King, Jr. Day	16	17	18	19	20
21	22	23	24	25	26	27
28	29	30	31			

February 2018

Sunday	Monday	Tuesday	Wednesday	Thursday	Friday	Saturday
				1	2	3
4	5	6	7	8	9	10
11	12 Lincoln's Birthday	13	14 Valentine's Day	15	16	17
18	19 President's Day	20	21	22	23	24
25	26	27	28			

March 2018

Sunday	Monday	Tuesday	Wednesday	Thursday	Friday	Saturday
				1	2	3
4	5	6	7	8	9	10
11 Daylight Saving Begins	12	13	14	15	16	17 St. Patrick's Day
18	19	20	21	22	23	24
25	26	27	28	29	30	31

April 2018

Sunday	Monday	Tuesday	Wednesday	Thursday	Friday	Saturday
1 Easter	2	3	4	5	6	7
8	9	10	11	12	13	14
15	16	17	18	19	20	21
22	23	24	25	26	27	28
29	30					

May 2018

Sunday	Monday	Tuesday	Wednesday	Thursday	Friday	Saturday
		1	2	3	4	5
6	7	8	9	10	11	12
13 Mother's Day	14	15	16	17	18	19
20	21	22	23	24	25	26
27	28 Memorial Day	29	30	31		

June 2018

Sunday	Monday	Tuesday	Wednesday	Thursday	Friday	Saturday
					1	2
3	4	5	6	7	8	9
10	11	12	13	14	15	16
17 Father's Day	18	19	20	21	22	23
24	25	26	27	28	29	30

July 2018

Sunday	Monday	Tuesday	Wednesday	Thursday	Friday	Saturday
1	2	3	4 Independence Day	5	6	7
8	9	10	11	12	13	14
15	16	17	18	19	20	21
22	23	24	25	26	27	28
29	30	31				

August 2018

Sunday	Monday	Tuesday	Wednesday	Thursday	Friday	Saturday
			1	2	3	4
5	6	7	8	9	10	11
12	13	14	15	16	17	18
19	20	21	22	23	24	25
26	27	28	29 YW: Shooting (Beehives) YM:	30	31	

September 2018

Sunday	Monday	Tuesday	Wednesday	Thursday	Friday	Saturday
						1
2	3 Labor Day	4	5	6	7	8
9	10	11	12	13	14	15
16	17	18	19	20	21	22
23/30	24	25	26	27	28	29

October 2018

Sunday	Monday	Tuesday	Wednesday	Thursday	Friday	Saturday
	1	2	3	4	5	6
7	8 Columbus Day	9	10	11	12	13
14	15	16	17	18	19	20
21	22	23	24	25	26	27
28	29	30	31 Halloween			

November 2018

Sunday	Monday	Tuesday	Wednesday	Thursday	Friday	Saturday
				1	2	3
4	5	6	7	8	9	10
11 Veteren's Day	12	13	14	15	16	17
18	19	20	21	22 Thanksgiving Day	23	24
25	26	27	28	29	30	

December 2018

Sunday	Monday	Tuesday	Wednesday	Thursday	Friday	Saturday
						1
2	3	4	5	6	7	8
9	10	11	12	13	14	15
16	17	18	19	20	21	22
23/30	24/31 New Year's Eve	25 Christmas Day	26	27	28	29

Notes

Notes

Notes

Notes

Notes

Envelope

DISCARD

CUT HERE

Fold onto next page and attach